J523 .8 2198219
BERGER, MELVIN.
BRIGHT STARS, RED GIANTS,
AND WHITE DWARFS /

About the Book

The galaxies are moving apart and the universe is expanding. That means that yesterday the universe was smaller than it is today. A year ago it was even smaller. And a million years ago it was smaller yet. It all started with an immense explosion called the Big Bang.

It is from that moment, some 13 billion or more years ago, that scientists now believe they can pinpoint the beginning of the universe and plot quite a complete picture of the life of a star. From its infancy as a protostar, to its maturity as a bright star, to its old age as a red giant, the star proceeds even further to a number of possibilities: white dwarf, supernova, pulsar or even the enigmatic black hole in space.

With dramatic photographs and a clear and thorough text, noted science writer Melvin Berger leads us through one of the most magnificent life cycles in our cosmos.

BRIGHT STARS, RED GIANTS AND WHITE DWARFS

MELVIN BERGER

G. P. PUTNAM'S SONS NEW YORK

Cover photo courtesy of
Celestron International, Torrance, California.

Title page photo of an exploding star
that creates a brilliant ring in the sky,
courtesy of Celestron International.

 Published simultaneously in
Canada by General Publishing Co. Limited, Toronto.
Printed in the United States of America
First Impression
Book design by Mike Suh

Library of Congress Cataloging in Publication Data
Berger, Melvin.
Bright stars, red giants and white dwarfs.
Includes index.
Summary: Describes the various stages in the birth,
life, and death of stars and discusses theories about
the ultimate future of our universe.
1. Astronomy—Juvenile literature. 2. Stars—
Juvenile literature. [1. Stars. 2. Astronomy]
I. Title.
QB46.B46 1983 523.8 82-23052
ISBN 0-399-61209-2

CONTENTS

The scientists said that the sun is growing larger and larger.

Hale Observatories

1 DEATH OF THE SUN

The year is J 4909. That is to say, it is the 4,909th year of the Tenth Era. It is just over 10 billion years since the sun and then the planet earth came into being.

For the longest time scientists had been telling the people on earth: "The sun is getting bigger and bigger. And it is giving off more heat. Soon it will become so hot that it will destroy life on earth. It will grow so large that it will swallow up our planet. We must make plans to escape."

But not many people paid attention. After all, science was very far advanced. People were living to be 300 or 400 years old thanks to artificial body parts that were available. Synthetic food and a clean man-made environment made life on earth very comfortable. It seemed that science could do anything. Almost everyone believed that scientists would find a way to stop the sun from becoming any bigger or hotter. People didn't think they had anything to worry about.

The sun kept swelling, however, and it grew more and more fiery. Its color changed from yellow to red. The added heat from the sun boosted the earth's average temperature. Every year it went up a fraction of a degree. Soon the edges of the polar ice caps began to melt. The level of the oceans rose, inch by inch. Many of the world's cities located along the coasts gradually flooded over. After about 100 years, all of the coastal cities had disappeared beneath the rising waters and the vast populations that had been living there were forced to move up into the mountains.

Still it grew warmer and warmer. People could no longer live in many parts of the earth. It was just too hot. Millions migrated to the polar regions, once barren areas under thick ice and snow, but now tropical jungles, filled with plant and animal life.

The sun kept growing larger, and the heat became even more intense. Thermometers exploded as the average temperature went up into the hundreds of degrees. The oceans and lakes seethed and bubbled like immense kettles of boiling water. Before, there had been too much water on earth. Now there was too little. The earth's waters were evaporating. Plants and animals could not live in these conditions. The earth was turning into a lifeless desert. The planet was becoming a burning-hot, bone-dry hunk of rock.

Within 300 years, almost everyone had left the planet and had gone to live in the "mobile homes" of the Tenth Era. These were space colonies orbiting around the earth. Some were on space platforms built by humans. Others were on asteroids that had been driven into position around the earth by powerful jet engines. These colonies were popular because they could be flown away from the sun as it got brighter and grew larger.

Over the following millions of years, most of the colonies were parked in orbits around the planet Mars. But as the sun continued to expand, Mars also became too warm. The colonies migrated through the asteroid belt toward Jupiter.

Finally, they arrived near Jupiter in the middle of the Eleventh Era, 11

As the sun's heat made life on earth impossible, people drove their space platforms out toward the distant planet Jupiter.

Celestron International

billion years after the creation of the sun and earth. The scientists in the space colonies were still keeping a close watch on the sun. They had seen it grow so large that it swallowed up the three closest planets—Mercury, Venus and Earth.

But now they noticed a change in the sun. Slowly it was beginning to shrink in size. The burning heat and blinding light were starting to fade. Over the next millions of years they found that the sun was coming back to what it had once been, giving off only as much heat and light as it had in the distant past.

With the return of the old conditions, the humans on the space colonies gradually headed back. They found a new planet had formed where earth had been before. It was similar to earth. They planted the seeds that had been passed down from generation to generation. They bred the animals that had been with them in space.

The sun, though, did not stay the same. It continued to grow smaller. Gradually, it gave off less heat and less light. On the new earth, the ice from the poles started to spread. Slowly the land was being covered with glaciers inching their way out from the polar regions.

As more water became locked into the advancing ice, the oceans again began to shrink. The population moved toward the equator to avoid the deadly cold of the rest of the planet. Some people returned to the space colonies and drove them toward the sun, looking for warmth and nourishment.

The sun grew smaller and smaller. As the ages passed, it turned into a tiny ball, not much larger than earth. It glowed with a white light. By this time all the humans—those on earth and those in space colonies—were long since dead. They could not survive without the sun's energy. Some space colonists had set off to find planets around other stars in the galaxy.

For 8 billion years the death throes of the sun continued. By the R Era, 18 billion years after its birth, the sun was completely dead. The sun was a frozen rock in space. So too were all the planets of its solar system.

This look into the future is, of course, science fiction. But it is not purely imaginative. It is based on what scientists already know about the life and death of stars like the sun.

Experts tell us that our sun was born about 5 billion years ago. It will continue as a bright star for approximately another 5 billion years. Then it will begin to grow larger in size and become red in color. At that point it will be known as a red giant. Over the following billions of years it will shrink in size and become white in color. That is the white dwarf phase. And finally it will lose all of its energy and become a dead rock.

But before we make plans to leave the earth, let's trace the birth, life and death of the stars. The story actually begins with the birth of the universe, somewhere between 13 and 20 billion years ago.

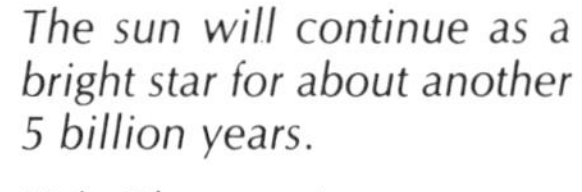

The sun will continue as a bright star for about another 5 billion years.

Hale Observatories

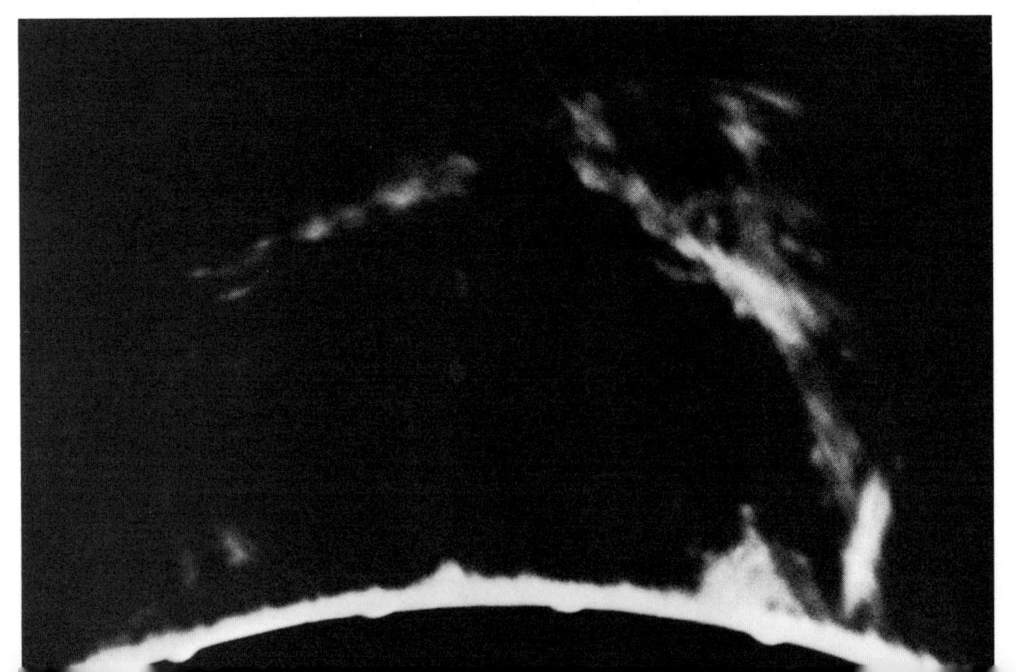

2 THE BIG BANG

When did the universe begin? How old is time? What is the size of the universe?

These are some of the questions that people have tried to answer for centuries. All religions of the world have grappled with these problems. And many scientists have put forth their explanations. In fact, one branch of science, cosmology, studies just the origin of the universe, and its past, present and future.

Out of all this thinking have come several different theories on the origin of the universe. Most cosmologists accept that it all started sometime between 13 and 20 billion years ago—they aren't able to give a more exact figure—and this is the way they believe it happened:

At the time of origin, all the matter in the universe was packed into one solid mass. This mass is sometimes called ylem, pronounced eye-lem. The ylem included all the original mass of the billions of stars, planets and galaxies found in space today, and everything in, on or around them. This mass was huge. Scientists guess that it measured about 7 billion miles (11 billion km) across.

The ylem was also superdense. So much matter was squeezed into this ball that a speck the size of a grain of salt weighed many tons. And it was at a very, very high temperature, probably in the trillions of degrees.

Then, suddenly, 13 or more billion years ago, the ylem exploded. The violence of this outburst was so stupendous scientists don't even try to describe it. They simply call it the Big Bang. According to most cosmologists, the Big Bang marks the birth of the universe and the beginning of time.

The Expanding Universe

Obviously there can be no direct proof of the Big Bang. But there is some indirect evidence that it took place. Certain facts and observations indicate that the universe is expanding. All of the galaxies seem to be speeding away from each other and moving farther out into space. An expanding universe makes a good case for the Big Bang theory.

The evidence for a growing universe springs from studies with a device called a spectroscope. When scientists look at light from a distant galaxy through a spectroscope they see a pattern, or band, of bright colored lines called a spectrum. The lines are caused by the different chemical elements found within the stars of the galaxy. Each element—hydrogen, oxygen, helium, and so on—produces a line or set of lines of a particular wavelength. Therefore the lines of the elements always appear in the exact same places on the band of light, and range in color from blue, for the short wavelengths, to red, for the long wavelengths.

About 1913, the American astronomer Vesto M. Slipher noticed that the lines from several galaxies were not in their expected places. They were shifted toward the longer, or red, wavelengths. This effect is known as the red shift.

Slipher and others explained the red shift as an example of the Doppler effect. Christian Doppler, an Austrian physicist, was the first to point out that as a source of light (or sound) moves toward an observer, the waves are squeezed together and made shorter. But when the source moves away from the observer, the waves are stretched out, or lengthened.

Have you ever been in a car when another car passes in the opposite direction with its horn sounding? As the other car approaches, the pitch of the horn seems to go up. As the car passes, the pitch seems to go down.

The same thing happens with waves of light. As the light source approaches, the waves are shortened. The spectroscopic lines are shifted toward the blue side. When the light source is going away, the waves grow longer. The lines are shifted to the red side.

Therefore, the red shift of the spectroscopic lines means that the galaxies are moving away from earth. Other studies showed that the galaxies are also moving away from each other. There is no discernible center to this expansion. Rather the entire universe is growing larger, or expanding.

By noting the amount of red shift of each galaxy, astronomers made another discovery. They found that the farther away the galaxy, the greater the red shift. Their figures made clear that the most distant galaxies were hurtling out into space much faster than the closer ones.

The galaxies, then, are moving apart and the universe is expanding. That means that yesterday the universe was smaller than it is today. A year ago it was even smaller. And a million years ago it was smaller yet.

Astronomers calculate the distance to the farthest galaxies to be about 80 trillion miles (128 trillion km), and the speeds at which they are moving to be about 136,000 miles (220,000 km) per second. Given these numbers, astronomers can determine how long ago the galaxies were all together and when they first started moving apart. *That* is the moment of the Big Bang.

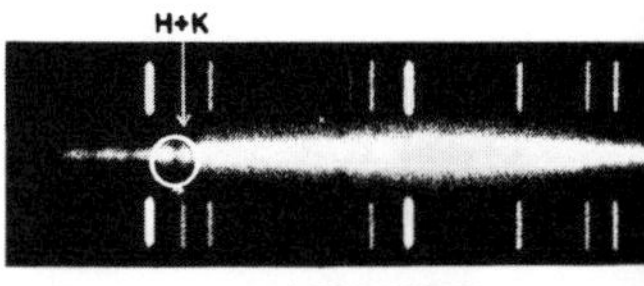

1,200 KM/SEC

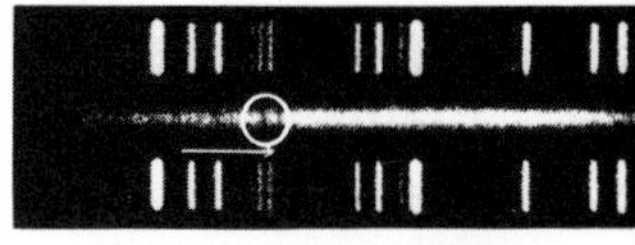

15,000 KM/SEC

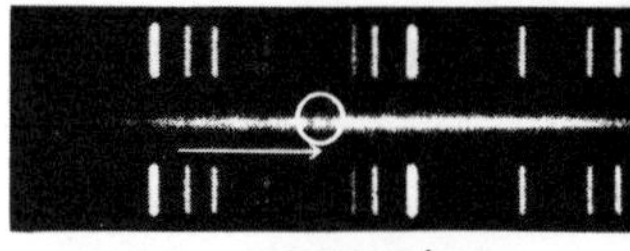

22,000 KM/SEC

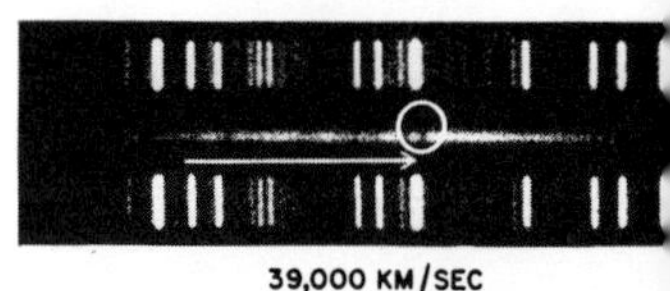

39,000 KM/SEC

61,000 KM/SEC

The little circle in the lens-like shape shows how two of the lines formed by calcium move toward the red side. Astronomers have found that the farther away the galaxy, the faster it is moving.

Hale Observatories

The most distant object ever seen in the sky is believed to be about 6 billion light years away.

Hale Observatories

Dr. Arno Penzias (left) and Dr. Robert Wilson stand in front of the giant horn radio receiver with which they picked up the background radiation.

Bell Laboratories

Background Radiation

Other support for the Big Bang theory came in 1965. At that time, Arno Penzias and Robert Wilson of the Bell Telephone Laboratories in Holmdel, New Jersey, were trying to learn what was interfering with radio signals on earth. No matter which direction they turned their very sensitive radio receiver, they picked up sounds of high-frequency radiation. They could not identify the source.

Robert Dicke, of Princeton University, offered a possible explanation. At the moment of the Big Bang, a fireball of high-energy radiation was flung out in all directions. It was like the radioactive cloud that spreads out after the explosion of an atomic bomb.

This cloud of radiation completely surrounds all the matter in the universe. As the universe grows larger, so does the cloud. It is just like a balloon being inflated with air. The background radiation surrounds the earth, and Penzias and Wilson were able to hear it as a hissing sound on their radio receiver. Since the radiation was all around the universe, they were able to pick it up no matter which way they turned the antenna.

After the Big Bang

An expanding universe and background radiation have convinced most astronomers that the Big Bang took place. Studies also seem to show that

As time passed after the Big Bang, vast clouds of hydrogen and helium gas began to form.

Hale Observatories

there were no complete atoms in the original ylem. An atom consists of protons and neutrons inside the nucleus, with electrons orbiting outside, all held together by their electrical charges. In the ylem, these particles, and many others, were completely separate from each other.

At the time of the Big Bang, the ylem expanded. It grew cooler. After about a million years, the temperature had dropped to about 5,000° F (3,000° K). (All temperature will be given in degrees Fahrenheit [F] from the common day-to-day scale, and in Kelvin [K] from the metric scale used by astronomers.) At this temperature, electrons became attached to protons, forming complete atoms of hydrogen. Mixed in with the hydrogen atoms was a small number of complete helium atoms. Each helium atom contains two protons and two neutrons in the nucleus, and two electrons outside the nucleus.

With the passing of more time, hydrogen and helium gas began to form into vast clouds. These gas clouds churned about, and like any clouds in the sky, they kept changing their shape. As they did so, some pockets of tightly packed gas were formed. These were small masses of denser gas within the large cloud. Even though they were small compared to the big clouds, they were still many billions of miles across. It was from these pockets of gas that the stars were later created.

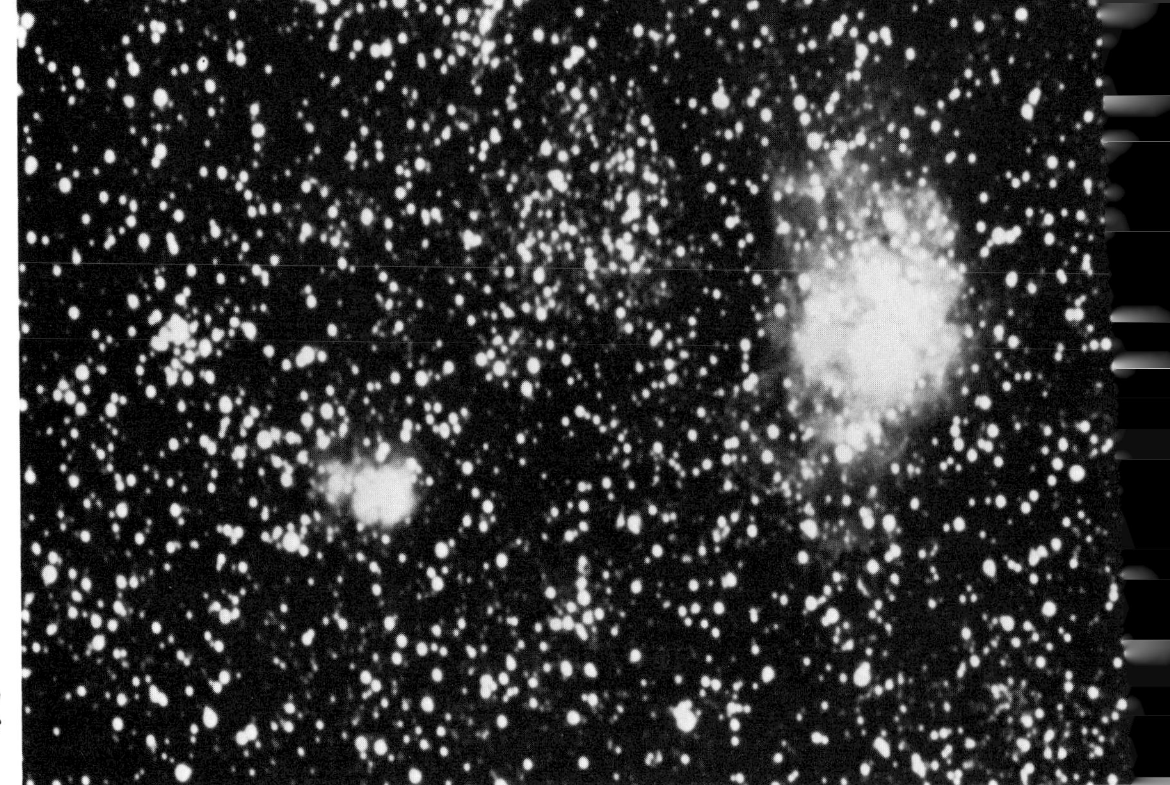

These large clouds contain the gas and dust that give rise to protostars.

Celestron International

Protostars are being born in this glowing cloud of gas and dust.

Hale Observatories

3 A STAR IS BORN

When an immense number of hydrogen and helium atoms come together in a pocket of gas, they become a unit, a separate cloud within the larger one. Such a unit is called a protostar. It is the first step in the birth of a star.

Protostars

Astronomers believe they have seen a number of protostars. These stars about to be born look like dark spots in the midst of light, glowing clouds of interstellar gas. The protostars are dark because there are large amounts of dust mixed in with the gas atoms. Some of these loose collections of hydrogen and helium atoms and particles of dust are several trillion miles in diameter. Then because of gravity, every atom and every bit of dust pulls on every other one.

The force of gravity in the protostar is like the earth's gravity with one difference: The earth's surface is solid. The objects and people on earth are held on the surface by gravity, but because of solidity of the surface they are not drawn down onto the earth's center. The protostar, however, being a cloud of gas, has no solid surface, so all of the gas atoms are pulled in toward the center from all sides. As a result, the protostar collapses. It grows smaller and smaller at a very fast rate.

Most of the collapse takes place in 1,000 years, which is a short time in the life of a star. The protostar begins with a diameter of perhaps a trillion miles. After the collapse, the diameter has shrunk to about 50 million miles (80 million km). The collapse is similar to a giant jet plane becoming the size of a grain of salt!

As the atoms in the protostar are drawn toward the center, they move faster and faster. Like any falling object, they pick up speed as they fall. As they move faster, they scrape and rub against each other. This friction, in turn, raises their temperature.

The protostar starts at a temperature of about 280° F (100° K). In 1,000 years the surface temperature is up to 7,200° F (4,250° K). At the core the temperature is perhaps 180,000° F (100,000° K).

At these temperatures, the hydrogen and helium atoms are moving at great speeds. They are not only being pulled toward the center, they are being flung about wildly in all directions. And they are colliding with each other with tremendous force. The electrons that are normally held in orbits around the central nucleus are knocked away. The atoms are shattered. They are broken apart into separate nuclei and separate electrons.

The heat created by the collapsing gas pocket is so great that the protostar glows with its own light. As the astronomers say, it is luminous. The protostar is now more luminous than the sun, even though it is not nearly as hot. Each point on the sun's surface gives off more light than each point on the protostar's surface. But since the protostar is much larger than the sun, the *total* amount of light that radiates from its surface is considerably greater than the light from the sun's surface.

After about 10,000 years, the protostar's surface temperature is up to

The newly-formed protostars glow more brightly than the sun.

Hale Observatories

about 7,700° F (4,500° K). The protostar is now 100 times as luminous as the sun. About 100,000 years later the surface temperature has risen to nearly 9,000° F (5,000° K). But all the while the protostar has been shrinking and it is now emitting only about ten times the light of the sun.

There is little change in temperature over the following 10 million years. The brightness, though, continues to drop as the protostar contracts. After a while, the protostar is actually less luminous than the sun.

During the next 20 million years or so, in the last stage of the protostar's development, its temperature rises to 10,800° F (6,250° K). Because of the higher temperature each point on the surface glows more brightly, and the protostar's luminosity rises again to that of the sun. The protostar begins to approach the sun in size too. It has a diameter of around 1 million miles (1.6 million km). Now the size of the star is fixed; it stops shrinking. It is set and stable. This moment, about 30 million years after the pocket of gas began to form, marks the birth of the star.

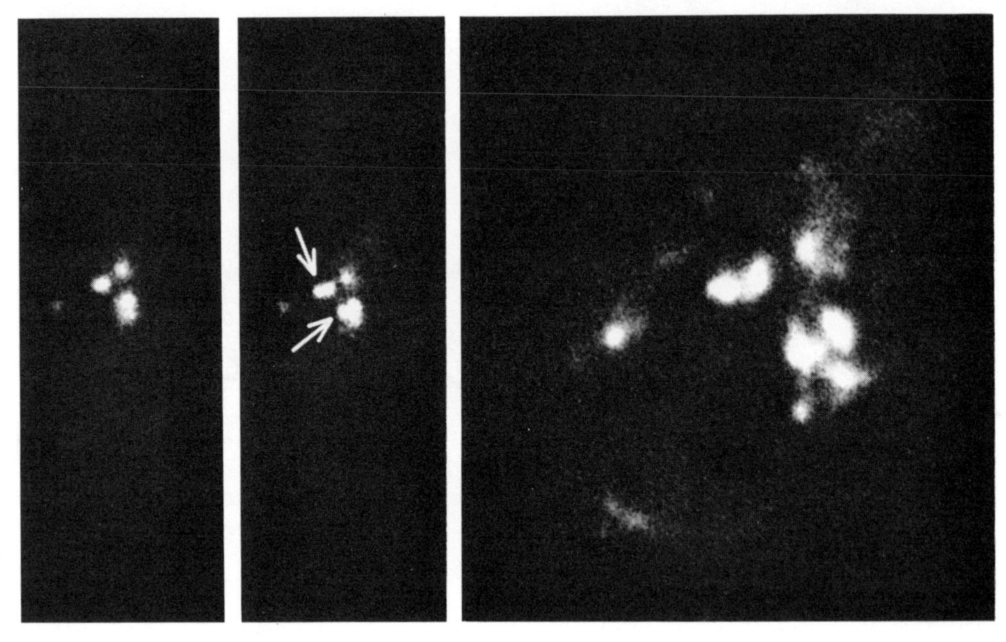

The three photos taken by George Herbig in 1947, 1954 and 1959 show the Herbig-Haro objects. They are believed to be protostars in the process of formation.

Lick Observatory

From Protostar to Star

It takes some 30 million years, then, for an average star, such as the sun, to pass through the protostar stage. But not all stars are average. There are many larger and smaller stars.

In general, the larger stars take a shorter time to pass through the protostar stage. For example, a protostar containing fifteen times as much matter, or mass, as the sun will become a star in about 100,000 years. The opposite also holds true. If a protostar contains only half as much mass as the sun, the process takes much longer. It may be 100 million years before such a protostar turns into a star.

Over the years, astronomers have observed a few stars being born. A series of photographs taken since 1947 of the constellation Orion seem to show the formation of new stars. They are now known as Herbig-Haro

The stars in the arms of the Whirlpool Galaxy are young and blue in color. The ones in the center are older and white.

Celestron International

objects. Others, called T Tauri variable stars, also show many of the characteristics of newborn stars. And any number of spots of higher temperature deep within large clouds of hydrogen gas might well be stars in the early stages of forming.

Stars of all ages exist in space. Some are old stars that came into being soon after the Big Bang. Many are stars that were created in the billions of years since then. And some are new stars just now in the beginning stages of life. All, though, developed the same way. They started as clouds of gas and dust that came together to form a protostar and went on to become a star.

4 BRIGHT STARS

A star is born when a protostar stops shrinking in size. At that moment the temperature at the center, or core, of the star reaches 18 million degrees F (10 million degrees K). Under these conditions a reaction, called nuclear fusion, starts in the star's core. It is nuclear fusion that separates a star from a protostar.

Nuclear Fusion

Nuclear fusion is the joining, or fusing, of small atomic nuclei to create larger ones. Basically, the nuclear fusion combines the nuclei of two hydrogen atoms to form the nucleus of one helium atom. As the fusion occurs, there is a great release of energy.

The hydrogen or H-bomb works on the principle of nuclear fusion. The powerful explosion of an H-bomb is the bursting forth of the energy from the fusion reaction. The fantastic amount of energy that pours out of an average star is like the continuous explosion of thousands of H-bombs.

The nucleus of the hydrogen atom is a single particle, a proton. Each proton has a positive charge. When two protons meet, they tend to fly apart. This is because like charges repel, or push each other apart.

The heat and pressure found at the core of young stars change things, however, making the protons dart about with tremendous speed. The protons travel so fast, in fact, that they overcome the force pushing them apart. When two protons collide under these conditions, they stick together. They fuse and become bound, one to the other.

As the two protons fuse, one of them emits a positron, which is a unit of positive charge, or a positive electron. With its positive charge gone, that proton becomes a neutron, a nuclear particle without electrical charge. At the same time a neutrino, a particle with neither mass nor charge, comes out of the reaction. The positron and neutrino, which are more like tiny bursts of energy than particles, carry away most of the energy released in the fusion process.

The neutron and other proton that are bound together form the nucleus of a deuterium atom. Deuterium is a heavy form of hydrogen, with a proton and neutron in its nucleus.

Now deuterium nuclei also become involved in the collisions taking place inside the core of the star. From time to time, a single proton bumps into a deuterium nucleus. They fuse. The result is a helium-3 nucleus.

Helium-3 is a light form of the element helium. It contains two protons and one neutron in its nucleus. Each time a nucleus of helium-3 forms, there is a release of energy in the form of gamma rays. Gamma rays are high-frequency electromagnetic waves that are similar to X rays.

The final step of the process occurs when two helium-3 nuclei collide. They fuse to form the nucleus of ordinary helium, or helium-4, with two protons and two neutrons. Since each helium-3 nucleus has two protons and one neutron, there are two protons left over. They are returned to the supply of particles for future fusion.

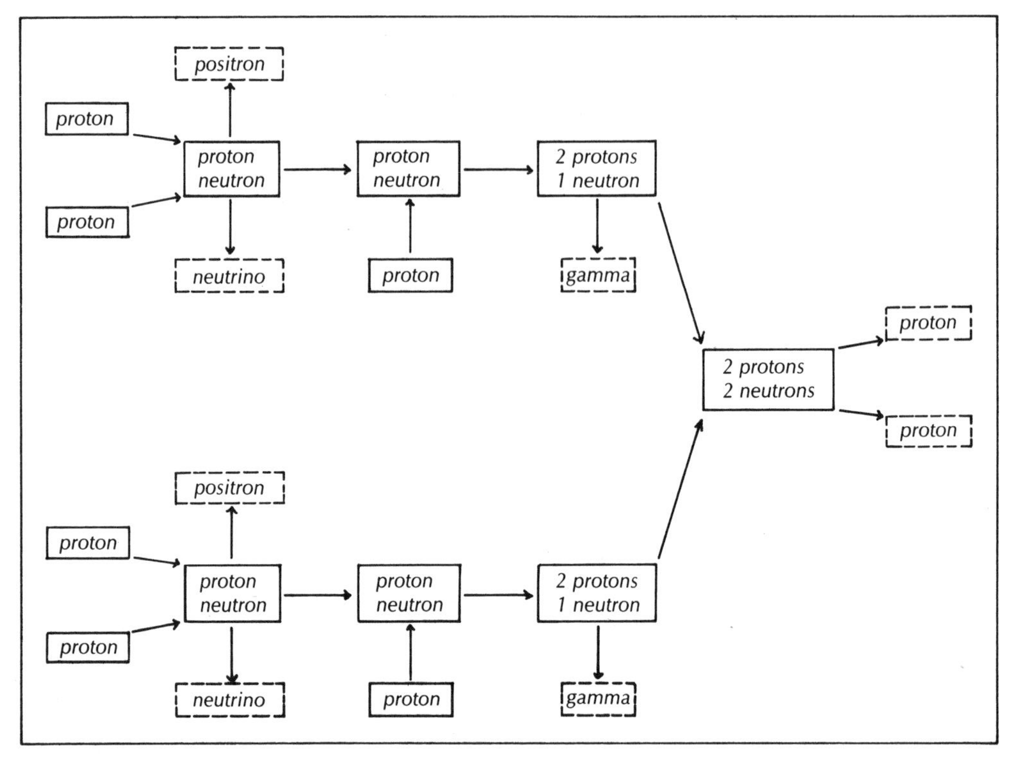

Fusion diagram

The three-step reaction by which protons fuse to form ordinary helium-4 is called the proton-proton, or p-p, chain. It may take up to 5 billion years for particles to come together to create a single helium nucleus. But the number of particles within any star is so immense that the process is going on all the time.

While the number of helium nuclei build up because of the p-p chain, other fusion reactions are also taking place. In very large stars, the reactions go through different steps. But in most cases, the main source of energy in stars is the p-p chain.

Loss of Mass

The p-p chain starts with four separate protons, in the form of four hydrogen nuclei. It ends with two protons and two neutrons fused together to form the nucleus of one helium atom. And in the process it releases a great deal of energy.

Where does this energy come from?

There is a loss of mass in the fusion reaction. Mass is very much like weight. It is defined precisely, though, as resistance to change of motion. It is this lost mass that is changed into energy.

For example, suppose that the fusion reaction takes place in 100 pounds (45.4 kg) of hydrogen nuclei. At the end there would only be about 99.3 pounds (45.08 kg) of helium nuclei. That is to say, 0.7 pounds (.32 kg) of the mass disappears during the reaction.

In his 1905 special theory of relativity, Albert Einstein was the first to explain what happens during the loss of mass. He arrived at the startling conclusion that energy and mass are closely related. And he showed that one could be changed into the other.

In working out the mathematics of this relationship, Einstein produced the most famous formula in all science, $E=mc^2$. Put into words, the formula says that energy equals mass times the speed of light (186,000 miles [300,000 km] per second) squared.

Thus, during the hydrogen fusion in the core of the star, the mass that is lost becomes energy. We can see the light and feel the heat energy pouring out of the sun. The same process is going on in every star in the heavens. Each of them is emitting a powerful stream of energy in all directions. We are not fully aware of this energy because all the other stars are so much farther away.

Astronomers have worked out the approximate fusion figures for the sun. Every second about 590 million tons (531 million metric tons) of hydrogen nuclei are fused into 586 million tons (527 million mt) of helium nuclei.

There is a mass loss of 3.9 million tons (3.5 million mt) every second.

Using $E = mc^2$, scientists can calculate the fantastic amount of energy radiated by the sun every second. The heat and light we sense on earth is only a very tiny fraction of this tremendous output.

The fusion reaction goes on for about 90 percent of the entire life span of the star. But the process cannot go on forever. The time it lasts is determined by the star's original mass and how much hydrogen it contains.

The sun is an average, middle-sized star. Right now it is still fusing hydrogen and creating helium at its core. About half its hydrogen is used up. It is expected to continue this way for just over another 5 billion years.

In stars larger than the sun, those containing more matter or mass, the fusion process speeds along at a faster rate. There are greater numbers of hydrogen nuclei. As they fuse, they release more energy, which brings over larger numbers of nuclei into the fusion process. On and on the process speeds, quickly using up the supply of hydrogen nuclei. Scientists guess that a star with ten times the mass of the sun will not last longer than about 10 million years.

In smaller stars, the process moves along more slowly. There are fewer nuclei to enter the fusion process and less energy is emitted. A star with only one-tenth the mass of the sun may continue hydrogen fusion for up to one trillion years.

The life cycle of a star has been compared to a human's life. The 30 million years as a protostar is like infancy or early childhood. In human terms, it lasts from birth to about 4 years.

The 10-billion-year period of nuclear fusion as a bright star is the time of youth and maturity. For humans, this would be from age 4 to 76. It is the longest stage for both star and human.

Then comes old age. But while mortals tend to grow smaller, the fading star grows larger. It becomes red in color. For these reasons, a star in old age is called a red giant.

5 RED GIANTS

The red giant stage comes near the end of a star's life. It is only a small part of the existence of a star. But it is very important. Red giants are necessary for the creation of the planets in the universe. Without red giants there would be no life as we know it.

The Turnoff Point

For most of a star's life, hydrogen nuclei are being fused into helium at its central core. As time goes on, more and more of the hydrogen is used up. After a while, the fusion process slows down and stops. There is just not enough hydrogen for the process to keep going forever.

The exhaustion of the hydrogen in the core signals the turnoff point, the star's passage into old age.

Without the hydrogen fusion, there is no longer a flow of energy out from the core. Until now, the outward pressure of the fusion energy balanced the inward pressure of gravity. Now gravity takes over. The core is squeezed and compressed. It grows much smaller.

By this time, most of the core is made up of helium, the result of the hydrogen fusion. As the helium in the core is compressed, it grows hotter. The heat radiates out to the shell of hydrogen gas around the core. When the core reaches a temperature of about 7.2 million degrees F (4 million degrees K), the nuclei of hydrogen in the shell begin to fuse. They form into nuclei of helium.

The hydrogen fusion in the shell around the core releases great amounts of energy. This energy carries immense masses of hydrogen gas out toward the surface. The star begins to grow larger, but its luminosity does not change. Astronomers call this a period of constant luminosity.

As the star grows larger, the gas it contains spreads out. This makes the temperature go down. It is the opposite reaction to the way gases become hotter when they are compressed.

The temperature at the surface drops to about 7,200° F (4,250° K). In that cooled down state, the star's color is no longer blue white. It now glows with a reddish color.

All the changes taking place in the star continue. The helium core keeps on collapsing. The hydrogen shell persists with the fusion process. The star grows still larger in size. And the surface gradually turns a bright red. In other words, the star has become a red giant.

Red Giants

Astronomers have tracked the lives of stars, such as the sun, from birth until they become red giants.

The sun was born about 4.6 billion years ago. It was somewhat smaller and less luminous than it is today. Until now it has been growing larger and brighter very slowly and gradually. Over the next 4.5 billion years, the process will continue, and the sun will gradually become bigger and shine more brightly.

When the sun is just over 9 billion years old, it will reach the turnoff

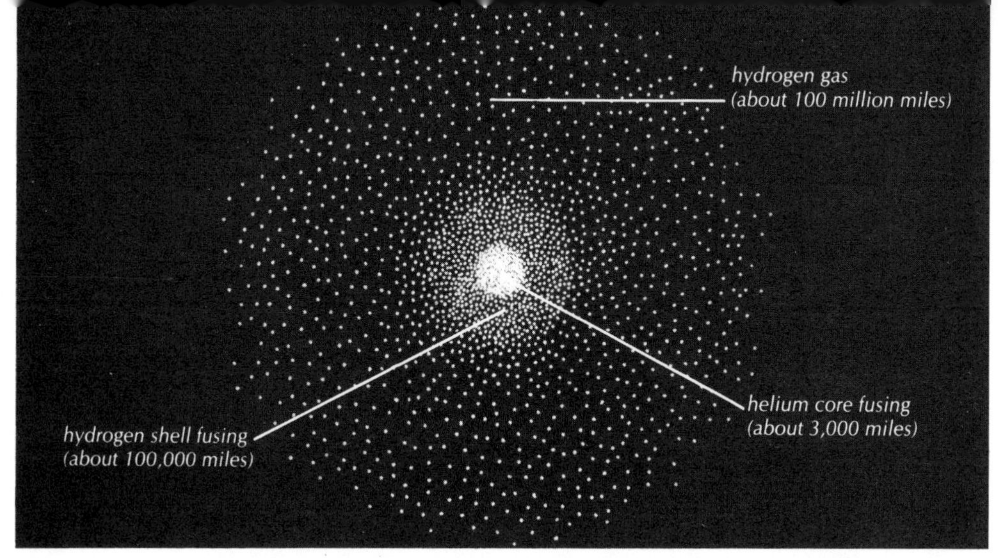

Diagram of a red giant

point. It will be more than 50 percent larger and twice as luminous as it was at birth. The sun will then enter its constant luminosity stage.

Once it passes the turnoff point, changes in the sun will begin to occur much more rapidly. Over the following billion years, the sun will double in size. Its luminosity will increase considerably.

During this time of expansion, the sun will swallow up the nearby planets, including Mercury, Venus and Earth. After about 10.5 billion years, the sun's diameter will be 100 times greater than it is now and it will be about 1,000 times brighter. It will be a red giant.

Astronomers have located a number of red giants in the universe. Among the better known ones are Aldebaran (in the constellation Taurus), Antares (in Scorpio), Arcturus (in Boötes), and Betelgeuse (in Orion). They are all large in size and red in color.

Most of the red giants are found in globular clusters. Globular clusters are groups of up to one million stars that move together through space. Globular clusters are a very late stage in the evolution of galaxies. Therefore, most of the stars in the globular clusters are quite old. Many were created early in the history of the universe. It is not surprising, then, that red giants, which are old stars, tend to be found in these clusters.

Most red giants are found in globular clusters, which contain up to one million stars. This globular cluster, found in the constellation Hercules, was formed 10 billion years ago, early in the history of the universe.

Hale Observatories

Helium Flash

Even after a star has become a red giant, the pressure on the core continues to build. The gas is so tightly packed that one cubic inch (16.4 cc) weighs one ton (0.9 mt). The core has a diameter of 20,000 miles (32,000 km), about twice that of earth. Yet it weighs almost 100,000 times as much as our planet.

Astronomer Robert Jastrow says that if a red giant were reduced to the size of a basketball, its core would be the size of the period at the end of this sentence. Yet, that core would contain fully 25 percent of the total mass of the star!

Because of the great pressure on the core, the temperature continues to rise. It gets up to around 180 million degrees F (100 million degrees K). At this critical temperature, a new phase begins. The helium nuclei begin to fuse. They fuse to form the larger nuclei of the elements carbon and oxygen.

Most astronomers believe that the main source of carbon and oxygen in the universe is the very hot cores of red giants. These elements make possible life in the forms we know it on planet earth.

What happens next is strange indeed. As the helium fusion keeps going, the temperature of the core rises ever higher. This speeds up the fusion reaction. The pressure builds. Finally, the helium core actually explodes. It is much like a super-powerful H-bomb going off inside the star. This uncontrolled blast is called a helium flash.

The energy from the helium flash, however, does not reach the surface of the star. No astronomer has ever seen a helium flash. But computer calculations leave little doubt that it does take place.

Right after the flash, the temperature of the core drops. So does the temperature of the surrounding shell. The rate of hydrogen fusion in the shell drops off. For the first time, the luminosity of the red giant diminishes.

With the falling away of the energy production within the star, gravity takes over. The star begins to shrink. For the next 100,000 years or so, the star gradually grows smaller and dimmer.

As the star collapses, though, the pressure on the core increases. The temperature of the core rises again. After another 10,000 years the temperature is up to about 360 million degrees F (200 million degrees K). The helium fusion starts again. The fusion process begins pouring out energy. The star is given a new burst of life. The drop in size and luminosity is brought to a halt.

All along, the helium in the core is being used up. Carbon and oxygen nuclei are taking its place. In time, the carbon and oxygen become the core of the star. When no more helium is left, the helium fusion at the core stops.

Once again, the force of gravity takes over. The carbon-oxygen core is reduced. Its temperature rises. This heats the surrounding shell of helium, which now starts to fuse.

The star swells in size anew, and it becomes very luminous. Its surface is red in color. At the end of only a few million years, it is a red giant once more. Now, though, the star is very near the end of its life.

6 WHITE DWARFS

We now know that a red giant is an old star that has already used up most of its supply of hydrogen and helium nuclei. The fusion process has slowed down greatly, or actually come to a stop. The star produces little or no energy. If it is an average-sized star, it is on its way to becoming a white dwarf.

Planetary Nebula

When the nuclear fusion has stopped, or almost stopped, no more heat energy is being produced. The star begins to cool. The outer layers of the star cool off first.

These exterior layers, like the rest of the gas of the star, contain atomic nuclei, protons and neutrons bound together without electrons. The electrons were driven off by the great heat. But now the nuclei are cool enough to combine with the electrons. As these nuclei capture the free electrons, they become full, complete atoms.

In the process of electron capture, there is a release of energy. This

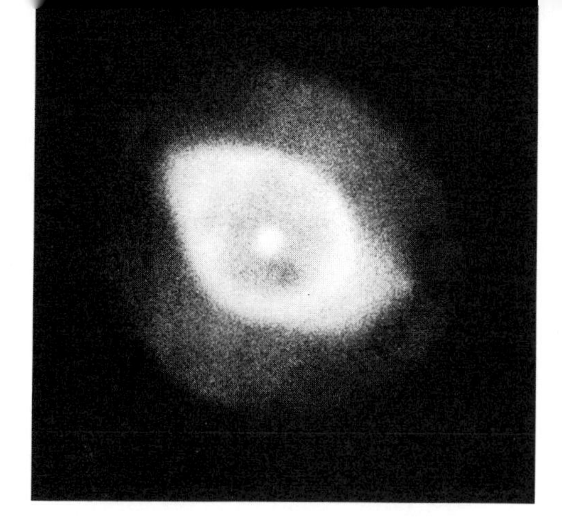

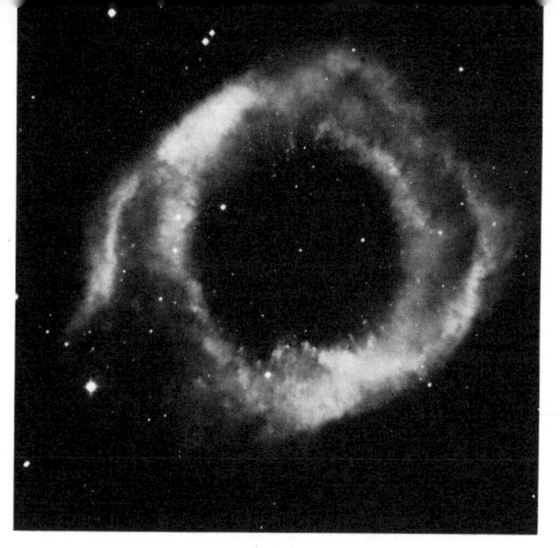

(left) The cloud of glowing atoms that moves out from the star is called a planetary nebula.

Hale Observatories

(right) The gas particles of the planetary nebula move out from the star at speeds of about 18.6 miles (30 km) per second.

Hale Observatories

energy radiates out. It raises the temperature of the star's outermost layer of gas. The heat causes this layer to expand.

The expansion triggers a runaway reaction. As the gas spreads out, its temperature drops. This allows more electrons to be captured by the nuclei. Still more heat energy is released. This further heats the enlarged outer layer. As it expands, its temperature drops. And so on and on.

The outer gas layer of the star stretches out farther and farther. In time, it becomes so big that it separates from the body of the star altogether. A cloud of glowing atoms moves out in all directions like a puff of smoke from a chimney.

To early astronomers, the envelope of bright gas given off by the star looked like a distant planet. They called it a planetary nebula, or a planetlike cloud. Today we know that a planetary nebula has nothing to do with a planet. But the name remains.

Planetary nebulas have a very short life, in terms of the universe. Scientists guess that they do not last longer than about 50,000 years. Just as the smoke from a chimney quickly disappears in the air, so the planetary nebula soon disappears in space. It quits the body of the star at a speed of about 18.6 miles (30 km) per second. The gas particles spread out over a vast stretch of space. Eventually they mix in with the clouds of gas normally found between the stars, and the planetary nebula is seen no more.

Reaching Old Age

With the planetary nebula gone, what is left of the star?

All that remains is a central core of tightly packed carbon and oxygen nuclei, and surrounding the core, a shell of helium nuclei. Some fusion still goes on in the small amount of helium that remains. But the star is quite different from what it had been. And it is about to change even more.

As a red giant, the star had been wrapped in a cool outer layer of gas. The surface temperature was about 6,300° F (3,750° K). Now the wrapping is gone. The core and shell are exposed.

The temperature at the surface now jumps to 90,000° F (50,000° K). Almost all of the energy that is produced in the shell escapes into space. There is not enough helium left in the shell to keep a fusion reaction going. Within about 1,000 years, the little remaining helium is used up. All fusion stops completely.

Lacking the outward pressure of the nuclear energy, there is nothing to resist the inward pressure of gravity. The star begins to collapse, bit by bit.

At this late stage in the star's life, all its material is packed into a shrinking space. It is like squeezing a large closetful of clothes into a small suitcase. The clothes are still the same, but they take up much less room. Likewise, all the matter that was in the large star is still there. Only now it is much more tightly packed.

The crowding and collapse go on until the once-giant star is roughly the size of planet earth. It has a diameter of perhaps 10,000 miles (16,000 km). All of the matter that was spread out in the immense star is now forced into this tiny sphere. Astronomers guess that a teaspoon of this matter weighs about 1,000 tons (907 mt)!

Even though the nuclear fusion process has turned off because there is no more fuel, the star is still very hot. It is white hot. Such a star glows with a faint white light. Because the star is luminous and because it is small, it is called a white dwarf.

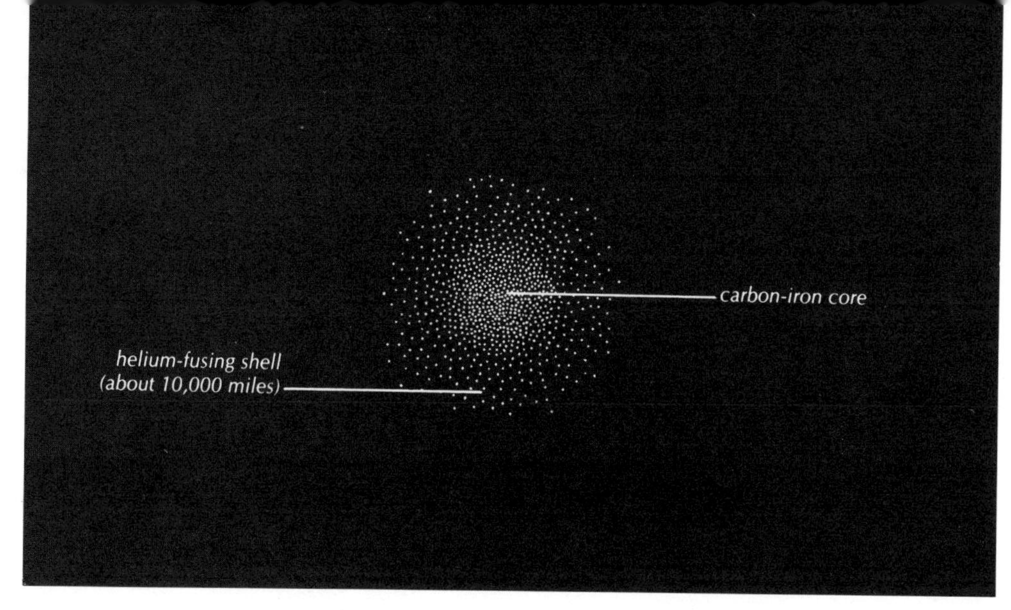

Diagram of a white dwarf

With the passage of billions of years, the white dwarf cools off. By degrees it changes from white hot to yellow hot. In time, the star cools down to red hot.

Finally the light from the star fades out. It becomes a dark, cold, dead lump in space. Some people call such an object a black dwarf. The black dwarf marks the end of the white dwarf stage, and the end of the star. Some astronomers guess that the sun will become a black dwarf about 18 billion years after it was created.

Astronomers have located about 500 white dwarfs. Since our universe is only approximately 13 billion years old, most white dwarfs have not yet cooled off enough to become black dwarfs.

Of the 20 stars closest to earth, two are white dwarfs. They are both companion stars. A companion is a star that orbits closely around another star. The two nearby white dwarfs are companions to the stars Sirius and Procyon.

The companion to Sirius, known as Sirius B, is the most carefully studied white dwarf. It is 10,000 times less luminous than Sirius. In size it is even smaller than earth, with a diameter of only 6,700 miles (10,800 km).

The surface temperature of Sirius B is around 54,000° F (30,250° K). This is, of course, far hotter than the surface of earth. But we still could not land on the white dwarf even when it cools down. Because of its high density, the force of gravity on Sirius B is a million times greater than on earth. If you weigh 100 pounds (45 kg) on earth, you would weigh 100 million pounds (45 million kg) on Sirius B. You would be squashed into a flat pancake at once!

During the fall of 1981, astronomers were studying a white dwarf in the constellation Ursa Major, the Great Bear. They had known of this star for about 20 years. Now, though, they found it had a surface temperature of about 180,000° F (100,000° K). This makes it the hottest white dwarf that is known. It has a mass about that of the sun. But it is all forced into a volume about the size of the earth.

The H-R Diagram

All the stages in the life of a star—protostar, bright star, red giant and white dwarf—can be seen on a chart called the H-R diagram. H-R is short for Hertzsprung-Russell diagram.

The graph is named for two astronomers, Ejnar Hertzsprung and Henry Russell. Working alone, each made a chart that placed a group of stars according to their luminosity and temperature. The more luminous stars appear higher up on the chart. The hotter stars are seen farther over to the left edge.

About 90 percent of all stars fall in a broad path across the H-R diagram. The path starts in the upper left-hand corner with stars one million times as luminous as the sun, and with a surface temperature of 72,000° F (40,250° K). Moving down and across to the lower right-hand corner are stars 1/10,000 as luminous as the sun, with surface heat of 5,400° F (3,250° K). The stars in this diagonal band make up what is called the main sequence.

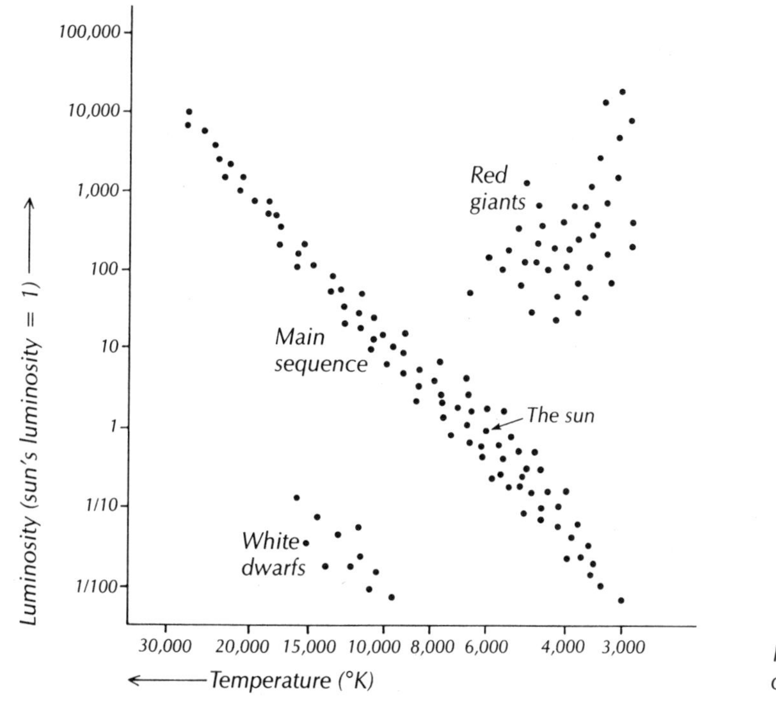

Hertzsprung-Russell diagram

The stars in the main sequence vary in mass. The stars at the top have about ten times the mass of the sun. Those at the bottom have a mass as little as one-tenth that of the sun.

The sun itself is located on the H-R diagram about two-thirds of the way down the main sequence. Since the luminosity scale is based on the sun, it has a luminosity of one. Its temperature is 10,800° F (6,250° K).

The red giants can be found in the upper right-hand corner. That is because they are high in luminosity and low in temperature. Located in the opposite, lower left-hand corner are the white dwarfs. They are low in luminosity and high in temperature.

Almost all the stars fit on the H-R diagram. Only a few do not. These are mostly stars that have much more mass than the sun. They start as main sequence stars, but as they grow older, they do not become white dwarfs. The fate that awaits them is far more spectacular. They explode into what are called supernovas.

A supernova is an exploding star that is much brighter than the original star, as can be seen in these two photos before and after a supernova explosion.

Hale Observatories

7 SUPERNOVAS

Some stars contain more than four and less than eight times the mass of the sun. These huge, massive stars face a far different old age than the smaller stars. They do not collapse and become white dwarfs. Instead, they are destroyed in fantastic explosions. They become exploding stars, or supernovas.

Scientists estimate that, on the average, there are about two supernovas in our galaxy each century. In each case, the star blows up with an immense release of energy.

This energy causes clouds of matter from the star to be driven out into space at speeds as high as 6,200 miles (10,000 km) per second. It also results in the star giving off a brilliant light. The luminosity of the supernova may be up to a billion times more than that of the original star. A supernova in a distant galaxy sometimes shines more brightly than the combined light of all the other stars in that galaxy.

Crab Nebula

On July 4, 1054, Chinese astronomers reported seeing a bright new object in the sky. They called it a "guest star." For several weeks it could be seen even during the daylight hours. In the dark night sky, it remained visible to the naked eye for nearly two years.

Modern astronomers have turned their telescopes to the same spot in the constellation Taurus where the Chinese saw the "guest star." They see a swirling, glowing mass of gas. It seems to be shooting out from some central point. Since it is shaped like a mammoth crab and it is a cloud, or nebula, they call it the Crab Nebula.

Scientists have made careful measurements of the size and rate of expansion of the Crab Nebula. Working backward, they find that the Crab Nebula must have started growing about the year 1054. What the Chinese called a guest star, then, was actually a supernova.

A large, though ordinary, main sequence star had been at that spot. No one noticed it or paid it any special attention. Then came the explosion. As the clouds of gas were flung out into space, the star changed from normal to unusual brightness. It was then that the ancients were able to see it. And now, more than 900 years later, it still is visible in the night sky.

The Explosion

Scientists are still not exactly sure how and why massive stars become supernovas. They have two possible explanations. One line of reasoning applies to stars with from four to eight times the mass of the sun, the other is for stars with about eight times the mass of the sun.

At the end of the red giant phase, all stars have a core packed with carbon and oxygen nuclei. Around the core is a shell of helium undergoing nuclear fusion. As the helium is used up, the fusion process stops. Gravity forces the core to contract.

In large stars, those with four to eight solar masses, the pressure on the core is immense. It is great enough to raise the core temperature to one billion degrees F (600 million degrees K). This is hot enough to trigger the fusion of the carbon nuclei in the core. The result is the creation of new, heavier elements, such as neon and magnesium. It also produces powerful surges of nuclear energy.

The energy raises the temperature in the core. More and more carbon nuclei enter the fusion process. It quickly becomes a runaway reaction, much like what happens in red giants just before the helium flash.

The pressure builds. Soon it reaches levels of perhaps trillions and trillions of tons per square inch. Then, with a shattering explosion, the star blows up. The material of the star is hurled out with a fantastic burst of energy. The explosion is like the helium flash, though much more powerful and violent.

The supernova explosion also reaches to the outer parts of the star. It does not just remain inside the core as it does in the helium flash. Few displays of nature are more spectacular.

With the explosion, the star becomes a supernova. All that remains of the original body is the tiny compressed core.

For those stars with around eight times the mass of the sun, the process is a little different. The heat of the core rises until it is measured in billions of degrees. Under this fantastic heat and pressure, larger and larger nuclei are formed by and enter into the fusion reaction. At the end, the core is packed full of iron nuclei.

The nuclei of iron cannot be made to fuse. They just grow hotter and hotter. In time, about one solar mass of iron is compressed into the central core. At this point, there is a tremendous implosion (the opposite of an explosion). With an immense heave, the iron core collapses completely.

The implosion releases a tremendous amount of energy. One astronomer

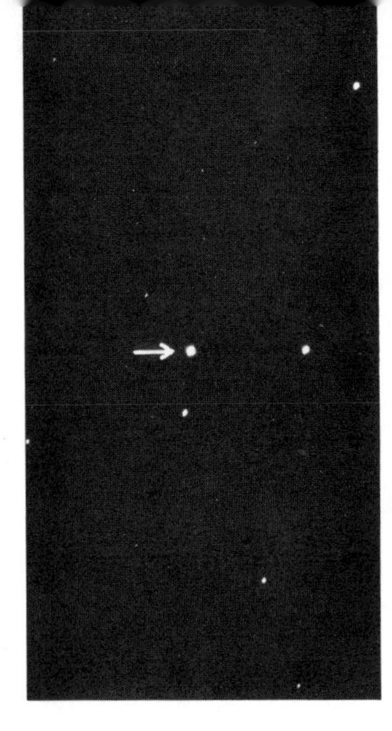

Just as a supernova becomes very bright all at once, so too does it quickly lose brightness. The lefthand photo, taken in August 1937, shows a bright supernova. The righthand photo, taken just 15 months later, shows how much fainter the light has become.

Hale Observatories

guesses that it equals all the energy radiated by the star during its entire lifetime. Like a coiled spring, the force builds up. Then, in a flash, it bursts out. It blows away all the surrounding matter of the star. Here too the result is a supernova.

In both types of supernovas, the violent outburst propels the matter at very high speeds. In this cloud are atoms of many of the heavier elements, such as carbon, oxygen, nitrogen, silicon, calcium and others. Some were formed by the nuclear fusion that took place during the life of the star. Some were formed during the short span of the supernova explosion.

In space, the matter becomes part of the gas and dust clouds between the stars. These clouds, which were formed at the time of the Big Bang, contain mostly hydrogen and helium. The supernovas add the heavier elements.

Later, when new stars and planets come into being, they will include the hydrogen and helium atoms from the Big Bang They will also take in the elements placed in the clouds by the supernova explosions. Probably, this is just how our planet earth was created.

Only four supernovas have been sighted in our galaxy over the last 1,000 years. Old writings tell of one found in the constellation Lepus in the year

1006. Then, as we mentioned, the Crab Nebula was first sighted in 1054. Later ones were found in 1572 in the constellation Cassiopeia, and in 1604 in the constellation Serpens. Most of the supernovas in our galaxy are probably hidden from view by clouds of gas and dust.

Astronomers have located a number of supernovas in other galaxies. Most have been found the same way. The astronomers compare photographs of the same region of the sky taken at different times. On rare occasions, they notice that one of the stars appears much brighter than before. That is often taken to mean that a star has exploded and become a supernova.

The obvious part of the supernovas are the giant clouds of gas hurtling out through space. But what about the small, squeezed down cores that are left behind?

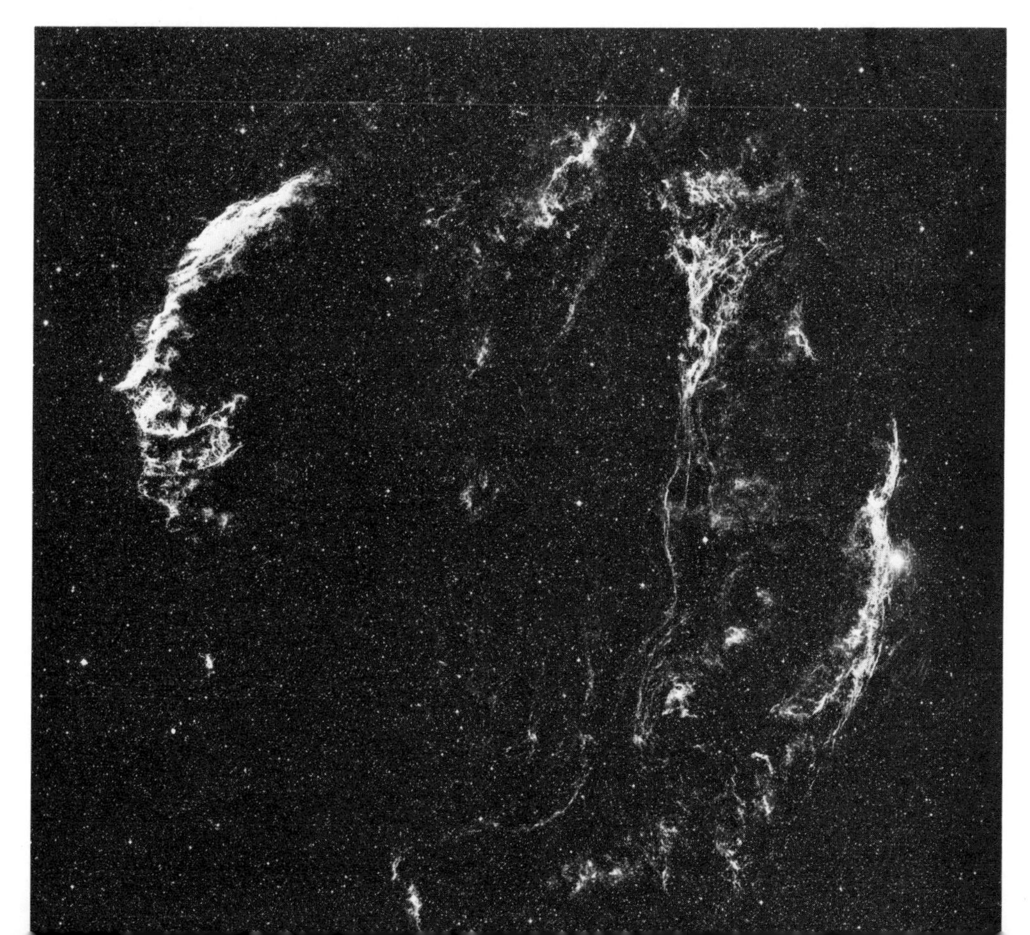

After a supernova has faded away, all that remains are giant clouds of gas hurtling out through space.

Hale Observatories

8 PULSARS

In 1967, Jocelyn Bell was a graduate student at the Mullard Radio Astronomy Observatory at Cambridge University in England. One day in August of that year, she was checking a chart of signals from space picked up by the radio telescope. A record of one radio signal caught her eye. The signal seemed to be flashing on and off about once a second.

Bell and the other astronomers tried to track down the source of this strange signal. Could it be from a radio transmitter on earth? From the direction, they knew the source had to be in space. Could it be from other creatures in space, or Little Green Men as they called them? There was no evidence that it was being produced by extraterrestrial beings.

Finally, they decided that the signals were coming from stars in our galaxy. Somehow these stars were emitting short pulses of energy that were being picked up by the radio telescope. The Cambridge astronomers named the sources pulsars, short for pulsating stars.

Bell's pulsar was located in the constellation Vulpecula. Each burst of energy from this source lasted 16/1,000 of a second. And the pulses came every 1.3 seconds.

Radio telescopes pick up natural radio signals that come from stars and galaxies in space.

National Radio Astronomy Observatory

Since then, scientists have found about 150 other pulsars. Some are in our galaxy. Others are farther out in space, in other galaxies. One pulsar was found right at the center of the Crab Nebula. A number have been traced to spots within other supernovas.

The findings raise several questions: What exactly are pulsars? Is there a link between supernovas and pulsars?

Neutron Stars

The astronomers' answers stem from an idea of the 1930s. Several scientists had worked out a possible sequence of events in a very large star, with about eight times the mass of the sun. They said that the core is made up of iron nuclei packed together. The nuclei are under colossal heat and pressure. Although the iron nuclei cannot fuse, individual atomic particles are forced to join together.

In particular, electrons and protons are combined into single particles. Since the electrons have a negative charge and the protons have a positive charge, the two charges balance each other. The result is particles with no charge at all. Such particles are called neutrons.

According to this idea, the neutrons in the core take up less space than the iron nuclei. The core collapses in an implosion and this leads to the explosion of the supernova. But more neutrons continue to be made. In time, the remaining core collapses down to a sphere with a diameter of 20 miles (32 km). Since it is mostly made up of neutrons, this body is called a neutron star.

A neutron star, then, is the leftover core of a supernova. Following this line of thinking, it should be very small. It should be extremely dense and also be rotating at a very high speed.

The original star was already rotating. As it contracted, the speed of rotation increased, just as spinning ice skaters, by pulling in their arms, spin even faster. Since the neutron star is only a tiny fraction of its former size, it should be rotating very fast indeed.

Finally, the neutron star should have a strong magnetic field. All stars have magnetism. But when this magnetism is concentrated in the very small volume of a neutron star, the field should become perhaps a billion times stronger.

If neutron stars are formed in supernovas, there should be a neutron star buried within the cloud of the Crab Nebula. Jocelyn Bell found a pulsar there. Since everything in the theory of the neutron star fits in with the observations of the pulsar, astronomers decided they are one and the same.

The proof lay in the pulsing signal coming from the center of the Crab Nebula. A neutron star has a powerful magnetic field. This magnetism causes beams of particles and rays to be emitted from the north and south poles of the star. As the star rotates, these beams sweep across the sky. Each

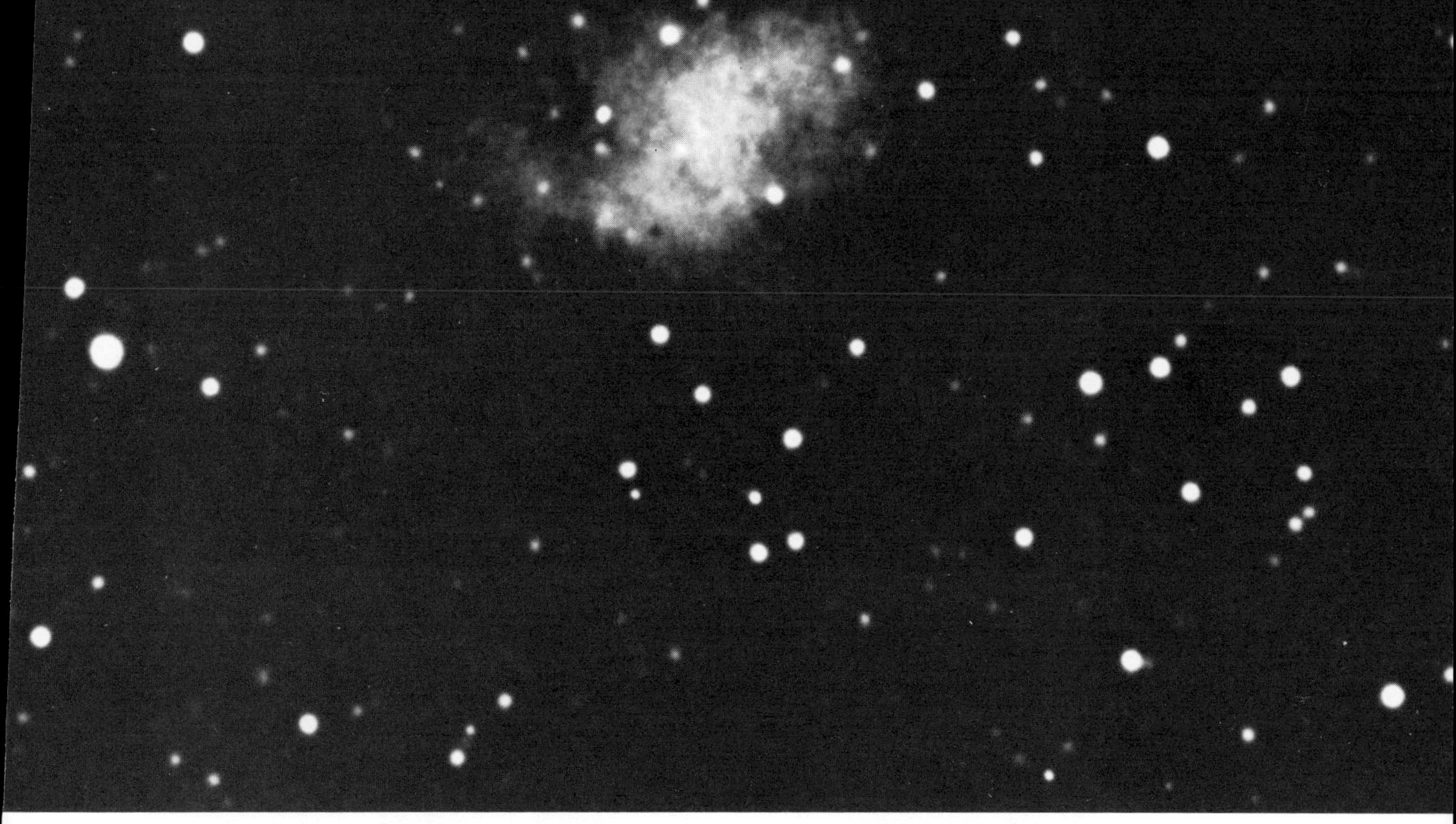

Astronomers believed that there was a neutron star buried in the cloud of the Crab Nebula.

Celestron International

time a beam strikes earth, it is picked up by the radio telescopes. The star pulses "on" as first one and then the other beam flashes toward earth. The "off" periods are in between, when both beams are facing away. This is like the rotating beacon in an airport control tower. To the person in one place on the ground, the beacon seems to be on when it is shining in his or her direction. But it appears to be off when it spins around and is shining in other directions.

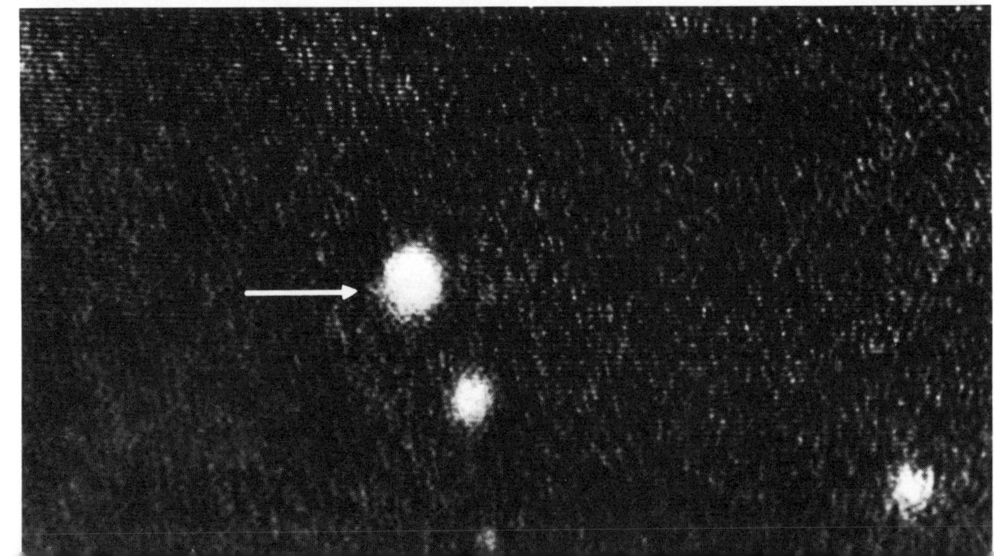

The pulsar flashes on and off both as a source of radio waves and a source of light. These two photos show the central region of the Crab Nebula. In one, the pulsar is shining brightly. In the other, it is not seen at all.

Lick Observatory

Astronomers also find that the pulsar in the Crab Nebula is small in size. The radio signals from this pulsar come at the rate of 30 times a second. They are always sharp, short and clear as received by the radio telescope.

If the pulsar were large, the experts would expect it to emit a wide beam of radiation. The signal would last longer, and some parts of the signal would arrive before or after others. It would, therefore, be blurred in starting and stopping.

Studies of the signals from the Crab Nebula convinced observers that they were coming from a small body. The scientists guessed it had a diameter of about 20 miles (32 km). This fits perfectly the earlier estimates of the size of a neutron star. It also strengthens the idea that the pulsar and a neutron star are the same.

Scientists are checking the pulsar/neutron star in another way. They would expect the speed of rotation of a neutron star to be decreasing very slowly. This is because the rapidly turning body throws off particles as it spins. Because it is losing mass, it should also be losing speed. By measuring the length of time between bursts of radiation, the experts can time the star's speed of rotation.

Very exact measurements now show that the time between the signals from the Crab Nebula pulsar is gradually becoming greater. The difference is very tiny, only 36.48 billionths of a second per day, but even such a tiny amount is considered significant.

With the discovery of pulsars, many astronomers were convinced they had unlocked the mystery of the final stage in the life of the massive stars. But recent findings show that this is not so. Under certain conditions, the core of a star may be squeezed into an even smaller volume. The star can be compressed to the point that it becomes one of the most amazing phenomena of the universe—a black hole in space.

9 BLACK HOLES

Black holes seem to belong more to moviemakers and fiction writers than to serious scientists. Many wild and fanciful tales are told about black holes. Have you heard about astronauts, space ships or even entire planets disappearing into black holes forever? Or about some people, who were drawn into black holes, and came out into a most beautiful and wonderful new universe?

Fictional accounts of black holes are no more fascinating than the facts that spring from recent research. The truth is that black holes really do exist, and are among the most remarkable findings of the universe we know.

The Biggest Stars

Black holes develop out of the biggest stars in the skies. These massive stars contain perhaps ten or more times as much matter as the sun.

An average, ordinary star has a mass no greater than four times the mass of the sun. Such a star, through most of its life, has a diameter of about 1 million miles (1.6 million km). At the end of its life cycle, it contracts to a diameter of perhaps 10,000 miles (16,000 km) to become a white dwarf.

Some stars are larger, containing up to eight times the sun's mass. Their diameters are also much bigger. After billions of years, these stars become supernovas, and eventually the core that remains is only about 20 miles (32 km) in diameter. Such a dense leftover core is a neutron star, or pulsar.

The biggest stars comprise ten or more solar masses. They are up to 1,000 times larger than the sun. Like other less massive stars, they too explode and become supernovas. But the immense pressure of gravity in such a huge star squeezes and compresses the core until it becomes a sphere that may be only 4 miles (6.4 km) wide. A tiny, superdense object like this, left over from a very large star, is called a black hole.

A black hole holds a huge amount of matter in very little space. Such a combination causes very unusual things to happen. Mostly they have to do with the force of gravity.

The strength of gravity depends,. in part, on the mass of the objects involved. In the black hole, so much mass is fixed in such a small body that the force of gravity is incredible. In fact, it is so strong that nothing can escape. Any planet, comet, asteroid, satellite or space ship that passes near the black hole is sucked in.

The black hole is black because even light is not able to get away from its surface. The immense pull of gravity keeps the light back. The same thing happens to other forms of energy, such as sound or heat. Anything that is in, on or near the black hole is stuck.

Evidence of Black Holes

Since black holes do not emit light, radio waves, or other forms of energy, how do astronomers know they exist?

Black holes reveal themselves by flashing out powerful beams of X rays. It is known that any matter that passes near a black hole is pulled into the hole. The closer it gets to the center of the black hole, the faster the particles of matter are moving.

The particles of matter are traveling at speeds of up to 62,000 miles (100,000 km) per second. As the particles rush in toward the tiny black hole, there are many collisions. These impacts, the scientists believe, create an X-ray beam that is emitted into space.

In December 1970, the Uhuru satellite was launched from Kenya. Its purpose was to search for sources of X rays in space. X rays were found to be coming from distant galaxies and from spots within our Milky Way galaxy. A few sources were picked up orbiting visible stars. But the most powerful source was one pinpointed in the constellation Cygnus. This source was named Cygnus X-1. The name means that it is located in Cygnus, and that it is the first X-ray source.

Astronomers turned their telescopes to the spot where Cygnus X-1 had been found. They saw nothing. But they did uncover evidence that there is something there.

Very close to Cygnus X-1 is a large visible star. This star appears to be behaving like a companion to Cygnus X-1. The two bodies orbit around each other. The astronomers' calculations tell them that Cygnus X-1 must now have a mass about eight times as great as that of the sun. This agrees with the model of Cygnus X-1 as a black hole. Suppose the star that became Cygnus X-1 started out at least ten times bigger than the sun and became a supernova. Then the remaining core might well contain eight solar masses.

Thus the experts now believe that Cygnus X-1 is indeed a black hole. It follows then that Cygnus X-1 is pulling matter away from its visible companion. A stream of gas is being sucked, at great speed, into the black hole. The particles of gas are bumping into each other with terrific impacts, and all these collisions are producing a powerful stream of X rays such as were detected by Uhuru.

Perhaps a dozen other X-ray sources have been found in our galaxy that are thought to be black holes, similar to Cygnus X-1.

Matter in the Black Holes

Most astronomers accept the existence of black holes. But now there is something else they want to know: What happens to matter that disappears inside a black hole?

One of the basic laws of nature is that matter cannot be destroyed. It can be changed in form; it can be converted into energy. But it cannot just disappear. This applies to all matter, including anything that is drawn into a black hole.

Scientists have come up with at least two wild, rather fanciful explanations of what happens. Neither one can be proven or disproven, but each is fascinating nonetheless.

According to the first theory, the matter passes into a tunnel, which the astronomers call a "worm hole." In the worm hole, the matter is turned into energy. At the end of the worm hole is a "white hole," a tiny body in space that radiates great amounts of energy. A white hole is the opposite of a black hole. The black hole draws in energy; the white hole emits energy.

Quasars are small, distant objects that are powerful sources of light energy. Could they be white holes in space?

Hale Observatories

The white hole sounds a lot like a quasar. Quasars are small starlike objects that have been observed in distant galaxies. They are powerful sources of light energy. Quasars are like stars, then, but they give off much more energy. Could the mysterious quasars really be white holes in space? This is a question that remains to be answered.

Other scientists, however, hold the second view. They believe that black holes lead to another universe. They think that the matter actually leaves our universe when it falls into a black hole—and comes out in a completely different universe, a universe that we cannot see or sense in any other way.

Modern astronomy, with its talk of black holes and white holes, and of worm holes leading to other universes, is changing our ways of thinking. Will these advances lead to exciting new understandings of the world in which we live? Or will they prove to be dead ends?

10 OUR COSMOS

Many mysteries remain in astronomy. Yet, scientists believe that they have quite a complete picture of the birth, life and death of stars.

Immense clouds of gas were created in the Big Bang. From time to time, more concentrated pockets form by accident within these vast clouds. Gravity then pulls these particles of gas together, creating a protostar.

When a protostar reaches the proper size and temperature for the fusion of hydrogen nuclei to start in its core it becomes a bright star. Great amounts of heat and light energy are emitted. Most of the billions of years of a star's life are spent in this phase.

The next stage in the life of a star comes when most of the hydrogen in its core is used up. The star enters its old age. It grows larger in size and becomes red in color. It is a red giant.

When there is no more fuel left for the fusion process, the star goes into its final phase. The dying star now follows one of three different paths. The outcome depends on the original mass of the star.

Most stars, which contain about the same amount of matter as our sun,

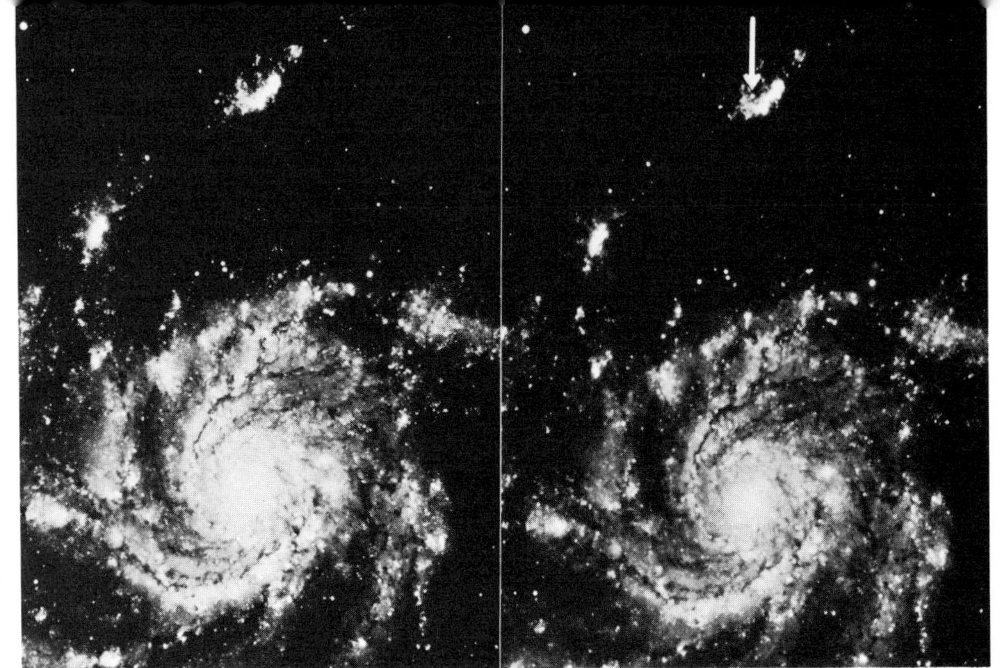

The larger stars explode as supernovas. These photos, taken 8 months apart, show a star bursting into sudden brightness.

Hale Observatories

fade away. They eject some matter as planetary nebula. Then they become white dwarfs. After they have completely cooled off, they turn into black dwarfs.

The larger stars blow themselves apart as supernovas. They end life as small neutron stars, or pulsars. The very largest stars also explode and become supernovas. At the last they become tiny, strange points in space called black holes.

Now that so much is known about the life cycle of stars, astronomers want to know more about the past and future of the universe. Most agree that it all began with the Big Bang. But there is less agreement on what the future holds.

One group believes that the universe will continue to expand without stop. Most evidence seems to support this idea. But it is far from an accepted fact. This so-called open universe model assumes that all the galaxies will continue to fly farther and farther apart. The clouds of gas between the stars will become thinner. Fewer new stars will form. The old stars will grow dim and fade. The universe will become dark and dead.

The other view is known as the closed universe model. It holds that the universe will only expand to some fixed size. Then it will start shrinking. All the galaxies and stars will then begin moving closer and closer together. After countless billions of years, all the matter will be gathered into one single mass of ylem. Ultimately, another Big Bang will start the process all over again.

No one really knows which model will work out. Perhaps neither. But one thing is clear. There is a need for more information in order to gain a better understanding of our universe. Perhaps with insight will come a higher regard for the cosmos and our place in it.

Hale Observatories

GLOSSARY

Astronomy The branch of science that studies the matter, including planets, stars, galaxies, and clouds of dust and gas, as well as the energy and forces found throughout the universe.

Atom The smallest part of a chemical element that has all the characteristics of that element. The atoms of different elements are made up of different numbers of protons, neutrons and electrons.

Big Bang The immense explosion that took place between 13 and 20 billion years ago, with which the universe began, according to one theory of cosmology.

Black dwarf The final stage of an average star, when it no longer emits any energy.

Black hole The remains of a giant star whose powerful gravity captures all nearby matter and energy, allowing nothing to escape.

Bright star A star in the lengthy, stable, middle period of its life, which lasts about 10 billion years.

Companion stars Two stars revolving around each other. Also called binary stars.

Constellation A pattern of stars as seen in the sky that has been given a name.

Core The central part of a star; usually refers to the region where nuclear fusion is taking place.

Cosmology The study of the origin, history and future of the universe.

Doppler effect A change in the wavelength of light or sound noted by an observer as the source moves toward or away from the observer.

Electron A negatively charged atomic particle that revolves around the nucleus of an atom.

Fahrenheit The temperature scale in common use. Absolute zero is −459.7 degrees F.

Galaxy A large collection of stars, made up of perhaps hundreds of billions of individual stars.

Gamma rays Rays similar to X rays, but shorter in length and with greater energy.

Globular cluster A group of up to one million stars, most of which are quite old.

Gravity The attraction of matter to matter. The greater the amount of matter, or mass, in an object, the greater its attraction to other objects.

Helium A chemical element with two protons and two neutrons in its nucleus and two electrons in orbit.

Hertzsprung-Russell diagram A chart that ranks and places stars according to their luminosity and temperature.

Hydrogen The simplest chemical element and the most important building block of the universe. An atom of hydrogen contains one proton in its nucleus with one electron in orbit around the nucleus.

Kelvin The absolute temperature scale used in astronomy. Absolute zero is 0 degrees K.

Luminosity The measure of the amount of radiant energy, such as light, emitted by a star or other body.

Main sequence A group of stars on the Hertzsprung-Russell diagram that runs diagonally from upper left to lower right. Most stars are on the main sequence.

Neutrino A particle with no charge emitted from the nucleus of an atom during nuclear fusion.

Neutron An atomic particle with no charge found within the nucleus.

Neutron star A small, very dense star made up entirely or mostly of neutrons.

Nuclear fusion The process by which heavier atomic nuclei are built up from lighter ones, releasing great amounts of energy in the process.

Nucleus The central part of an atom, containing protons and neutrons. Electrons revolve around the nucleus.

P-P chain A type of nuclear fusion.

Planet A large body that does not produce its own heat or light, found in orbit around a central star.

Planetary nebula A shell of glowing gas surrounding a star that was ejected from that star.

Positron An atomic particle similar to an electron, but with a positive charge and almost no mass.

Proton An atomic particle with a positive charge; found in the nucleus of the atom.

Protostar The original material from which a star will develop when the hydrogen fusion process starts.

Pulsar A small object in space, probably a neutron star, that emits regular pulses of radio waves.

Quasar A distant starlike object that appears to emit more light than an entire galaxy.

Red giant A large, luminous star with a cool surface, and therefore red in color.

Red shift The shift toward the red, or longer, wavelengths of light in the spectrum of a star; believed to be caused by the Doppler effect.

Spectroscope A device that separates light, such as the light from a star or galaxy, into a rainbowlike band of colors called a spectrum.

Star A large sphere of gas that emits energy because of the nuclear fusion going on in its interior.

Sun The nearest star to earth, around which earth and the other planets of our solar system revolve.

Supernova An exploding star that suddenly becomes much more luminous.

Universe All matter and energy, and the space in which they are found.

White dwarf A small, hot star near the end of its nuclear fusion period.

White hole According to one theory, the place where the matter and energy that disappeared in a black hole returns to our universe.

Worm hole A possible connection between two universes, or between a black hole and a white hole.

X rays Invisible rays that can pass through some matter. Some objects in space emit X rays.

Ylem All the material of the universe at the time of the Big Bang.

INDEX